Go Away!

By Janine Amos   Illustrated by Annabel Spenceley

Consultant Rachael Underwood

Gareth Stevens Publishing
A WORLD ALMANAC EDUCATION GROUP COMPANY

Please visit our web site at: www.garethstevens.com
For a free color catalog describing Gareth Stevens Publishing's
list of high-quality books and multimedia programs, call
1-800-542-2595 (USA) or 1-800-387-3178 (Canada).
Gareth Stevens Publishing's fax: (414) 332-3567.

Library of Congress Cataloging-in-Publication Data

Amos, Janine.
    Go away! / by Janine Amos; illustrated by Annabel Spenceley.
      p. cm. — (Courteous kids)
    Includes bibliographical references.
    Summary: Two brief stories demonstrate the importance of looking at a situation
from another person's point of view when both of you want the same thing.
    ISBN 0-8368-3607-3 (lib. bdg.)
    1. Social interaction in children—Juvenile literature. 2. Problem solving
in children—Juvenile literature. [1. Problem solving. 2. Behavior. 3. Conduct
of life.] I. Spenceley, Annabel, ill. II. Title.
BF723.S62A467   2003
177'.1—dc21   2002036478

This edition first published in 2003 by
Gareth Stevens Publishing
A World Almanac Education Group Company
330 West Olive Street, Suite 100
Milwaukee, Wisconsin 53212 USA

3 1984 00204 7478

Series editor: Dorothy L. Gibbs
Graphic designer: Katherine A. Goedheer
Cover design: Joel Bucaro

This edition © 2003 by Gareth Stevens, Inc. First published by Cherrytree Press,
a subsidiary of Evans Brothers Limited. © 1999 by Cherrytree (a member of the
Evans Group of Publishers), 2A Portman Mansions, Chiltern Street, London
W1U 6NR, United Kingdom. This U.S. edition published under license from
Evans Brothers Limited. Additional end matter © 2003 by Gareth Stevens, Inc.

Printed in the United States of America

1 2 3 4 5 6 7 8 9 07 06 05 04 03

Note to Parents and Teachers

The questions that appear in **boldface** type can be used to initiate
discussion with your children or class. Encourage them to think of
possible answers before continuing with the story.

Grandma's Story

Ben is watching a caterpillar.

Grandma is reading a story to Chen and Luke.

Ben decides he wants to hear the story, too.
Ben goes over to Grandma.

He crawls over Luke to get
onto Grandma's lap.

7

"Go away!" Luke shouts.

How do you think Ben feels?

"Now, Luke," says Grandma,
"I think Ben wants to listen, too."

10

"But I was here first," says Luke.

Grandma smiles.
"You all want to sit on my lap!" she says.

"I wish I had a giant's lap!" says Grandma.
What do you think they could do?

"I'll sit next to you, Grandma,"
says Chen, "and Ben can sit on my lap."

14

"OK!" says Ben.
How do you think Ben feels now?

"Now we have two laps
to share!" says Grandma.

Nadia's Store

Nadia is making a store.
She sets out apples, eggs, and bread.

Here comes Maggie.
"I'll be the storekeeper," she says.
"You can buy my things."

Maggie picks up some stones.
"These can be the money," she says.

"Go away!" Nadia shouts.
How do you think Maggie feels?

Steve comes over.
"You sound upset, Nadia," he says.
"What is Maggie doing that you don't like?"

"She wants to be the storekeeper,"
says Nadia, "but I'm the storekeeper!"

"I want to sell things, too!" says Maggie.

"Hmmm," says Steve, "so you
both want to be the storekeeper."

25

"Yes," says Maggie.
Nadia nods.
What do you think they could do?

"We could have two storekeepers," says Nadia.

"But who would be the customer?" asks Maggie.

Maggie looks at Nadia.
Nadia looks at Maggie.

Nadia and Maggie look at Steve.

"Steve would!" they both shout.
How do you think Steve feels?

31

Saying "Go away!" lets people know that you don't like what they're doing, but it can also make people feel upset. Instead, think about what you would like and tell the other person. If you both want different things, try to solve the problem by talking about it.

More Books to Read

Badger's Bad Mood. Hiawyn Oram (Scholastic)

Go Away, Shelley Boo! Phoebe Stone
(Little, Brown and Company)

How to Lose All Your Friends. Nancy Carlson
(Econo-Clad Books)